CLEVELAND RADIO PLAYERS

Published by Cleveland Radio Players

Copyright © 2015 by Milton Matthew Horowitz

All rights, including the right of reproduction in whole or in part, in any form, including digital reproduction, are reserved. Published in the United States by Cleveland Radio Players.

CAUTION: Professionals and amateurs are hereby warned that *Fall Out Guys*, being fully protected under the Copyright Laws of the United States is subject to royalty. All rights, including professional, amateur, motion picture, recitation, lecturing, public reading, radio and television broadcasting, and the rights of translation into foreign languages, are strictly reserved. Particular emphasis is laid on the question of readings, permission for which must be secured in writing from the author's representative at Cleveland Radio Players, 2218 Superior Ave, Suite 203, Cleveland, OH 44114. The amateur acting rights of *Fall Out Guys* are controlled exclusively for the author by the author's representative.

ISBN-13: 978-0692360323 (Cleveland Radio Players, The)

Original adaption and Performances

Originally adapted for the radio and performed by The Cleveland Radio Players. Directed by Milton Matthew Horowitz. Recorded at Bad Racket Studios.

Starring:

Cory Shy	Narrator
Logan Smith	Guy
Milton Matthew Horowitz	Buddy
Denny Castiglione	Emergency Public Safety Notice
Deanna Dionne	Emergency Frequency Voice #1
Kat Bi	Emergency Frequency Voice #2

Fall out Guys

Seven Years Of Fallout

Milton Matthew Horowitz

The Cleveland Radio Players   www.clevelandradioplayers.com
2218 Superior Ave #203   theradioplayers@gmail.com
Cleveland Ohio 44114   2162694171

FALL OUT GUYS

CHARACTERS

WOMEN

          EMERGENCY FREQUENCY
This is to be played by a woman representing The United State Government extraction team.

          NARRATOR
   (optional)
The narrator may or may not be played by a woman depending on whether or not the narrator is included on stage.

MEN

          GUY
Guy is a doomsday prepper and owns the fallout shelter that helps him survive the apocalypse.

          BUDDY
Buddy is a bit of a wanderer and winds up finding Guy at the escape hatch of his fallout shelter just prior to the dropping of the bomb. Buddy is a bit of a stoner and was once a pool cleaning guy.

          NARRATOR
   (optional)
The narrator may or may not be played by a man depending on whether or not the narrator is included on stage.

ACT I

SCENE 1

          (Sounds of AIR RAID SIRENS and PEOPLE PANICKING is all you can hear in the distance. The sounds of an upbeat jazz recording from the same era as old nuclear testing fills the airwaves as a PUBLIC SERVICE ANNOUNCEMENT warns people of the impending doom.)

AIR RAID SIRENS BLARE IN THE DISTANCE

PEOPLE PANICKING/MOB OR RIOTS SFX

MUSIC CUE: UPBEAT JAZZ MUSIC

EMERGENCY PUBLIC SAFETY NOTICE

PUBLIC SAFETY NOTICE
(v.o./recording)
TAKE COVER!... Be prepared with the backyard family fallout shelter in cold war America... You can protect your family against fallout with the Kelsey-Hayes company fallout shelter... IMPERVIOUS TO RADAR and GUARANTEED AIRTIGHT!... Learn how to protect yourself from atomic bombing... Every bunker comes with a lead-clad steel hatch, air filter, periscope, air exhaust pump, plumbing, ladder, emergency oxygen, food and water storage for 7 years, spare batteries, and a Geiger counter... Order yours while supplies last...

FADE PUBLIC SERVICE ANNOUNCEMENT

MUSIC DIPS

NARRATOR
Ya know when we first started testing nuclear weapons, we realized, right away, what a powerful device we created... Certainly we all hoped nobody would be stupid enough to use 'em... Ah those were the good ol' days, when we blew shit up and intentionally let video footage leak out so our enemies would get their hands on it and fear us as the awesome destructive force that we are (chuckles)... And if someone got out of line you just drop a little boom boom on 'em... Fuck up their area with radiation for a while... Yeahhhh but that could only last for so long... Just sittin' on weapons, waitin' to blow shit up.... Well we built 'em didn't we? We got to use 'em someday... Oh

> NARRATOR
> that's today, didn't I tell you? Yeah, the world's gone fuckin' nuts these last few weeks, Al-Qaeda finally got good with that internet shit and somehow they hacked every country's launch codes... Least we knows it's comin' this time. Some people are prepared, some not so much. It should be here any minute though... So gather in what ya can while ya still can... Take a moment to reflect upon something that might be worth reflectin' upon. Try to think of something nice. I mean after all it is a grinnin'-ass world... and I wanna go out with a smile.

> MUSIC CUE: OVERLY POSITIVE MUSIC SWELLS
>
> FADE MUSIC OUT

EXT.DAY FIELD OUTSIDE BOMB SHELTER DOOR

> PEOPLE PANICKING/MOB OR RIOTS SFX
>
> AIR RAID SIRENS IN THE DISTANCE

> NARRATOR
> People are scattering with luggage and coolers and shit... In the ground is a hole with a partial ladder sticking out. GUY is going over his checklist one last time and taking one last look at the sun when BUDDY approaches.

> BUDDY
> Hay man do you have a shelter? Do you have room in your shelter? I don't have anywhere to hunker down and we don't have much time left!

> GUY
> I mean... I have room... But... I don't know?

> BUDDY
> What do you mean you don't know? Come on man I'll die out here... Don't you have any compassion?

GUY
Compassion has nothing to do with it, it's just that I hardly know you. I mean I just met you as of now.

BUDDY
Yeah, well, I mean it's not like I have much of a choice here, I just wanna live.

GUY
Yeah well, I mean, I don't know anything about you and fallout is 7 years... That's 7 years I have to spend with you... I don't know how I feel about that.

BUDDY
Please man, I won't be a bother and if ya don't like me you can kick me out after the blast if you want!

GUY
And open the sealed hatch and risk contaminating my shelter... No way... Not an option... Suppose you tell me a little about yourself first...

BUDDY
Are you serious?

GUY
Yeah man 7 years is a serious commitment .

BUDDY
Ok... I um... am a city activist and worked on the Obama campaign.

GUY
(in disapproval)
Ehhhh...

BUDDY
Uh ok I uh... I can do lots of card tricks.

GUY
(indifferent)
MMMMM...

                    BUDDY
          I have 6 pounds of weed in this
          trash bag and a cat that can catch
          playing cards.

                    GUY
          Ok you're in... Come on take one
          last look at the sun... It's gonna
          be a long time before we get to
          look at it again...

                    NARRATOR
          Buddy takes a picture of the sun
          like a dummy and they begin to
          descend on the ladder into the
          ground.

                                        FADE OUT:

                              AIR RAID SIRENS SWELL

                        EMERGENCY FREQUENCY WARNING

                                        FADE OUT

                              ATOMIC BOMB EXPLOSIONS

                                    EARTH SHAKING

                                          SILENCE

SCENE 2 INT. BOMBSELTER

                              FADE IN BOMB SHELTER ENVIRONMENT

                    NARRATOR
          Scene 2...The two men are sitting
          on the ground rising from tornado
          shelter posture as soot falls from
          the ceiling and ground shakes below
          them. Lights flicker but then hold
          steady...

                    GUY
          Well that's it... Seven years
          starts right now...

                    NARRATOR
          Guy starts setting a bunch of
          clocks on a nearby shelf to the
          time on his wristwatch
          synchronizing all the clocks to the
          time on the surface.

FAINT CLOCKS TICKING

BUDDY
Yeah I notice you have a lot of clocks... Whats with all the clocks?

GUY
It's important we know what time it should be on the surface so we can try to live as normal lives as we can while we're down here... Come on, help me set all these clocks...

BUDDY
I mean, but does it really matter anymore? And this doesn't make sense, shouldn't we save some of the clocks to set later for when the ones we set now die?

GUY
I have extra batteries for all the clocks. I don't wanna risk anything. We'll just keep changing the batteries as they die.

BUDDY
Yeah, but suppose they all die at the same time. It just sounds like a waste of batteries.

GUY
Look. I have a plan and we lived this long, so lets just stick to it.

BUDDY
I have another question... Whats with all these costumes here? You have like 100 costumes.

GUY
That, too, is so we can try to live as normal of a life as we can.

BUDDY
I don't think I follow.

GUY
Look, people take everyday routine life for granted. And this way, with these costumes we can try to

GUY
strive for a manner of living that can resemble that of life on the surface.

BUDDY
How do you mean?

GUY
Here, just humor me for a second... Let's just say I had to go to the grocery... I would tell you... Hey, I'm going out to the grocery store to get us some food. I'll back in a jiff...

NARRATOR
Buddy stands there blank-faced and does not understand.

GUY
I said! ... I have to go to the grocery. (motions towards the rack of costumes)

BUDDY
Oh right, right, I get ya.

NARRATOR
Buddy quickly puts on a costume that resembles that of a grocery clerk while Guy pretends to be shopping around.

GUY
Oh well, hello, good day to you sir... Fine day, is it not?

BUDDY
Oh yeah, nicer than yesterday I would say.

GUY
Yeah, I would say... I got a new roommate today, so I thought I'd pick us up some nice food to celebrate.

BUDDY
Fantastic choices sir, I'm sure your new roommate will be impressed... Will this be all for you today sir?

GUY
Why yes, that will be all for today.

BUDDY
Thanks, come again...

GUY
I'll be back tomorrow... I have to make it to the post office before it closes.

NARRATOR
Buddy doesn't pick up on Guy's hinting...

GUY
I said... I have to make it to the POST OFFICE before it closes...

BUDDY
Oh right, right, I gotcha...

NARRATOR
Buddy shuffles through the rack of costumes and finds the mail room attendant hat and matching carrier bag.

GUY
Hello... sir.

BUDDY
Good day to you sir... Welcome to the post office... How can I help you.

GUY
Well, I have to send in an insurance claim to my claims adjuster... Ya see my house was destroyed in an end-of-the-world type catastrophe.

BUDDY
Oh I'm sorry to hear that sir... I'll make sure this gets to its destination right away...

GUY
Be sure that you do... I don't want any unexpected delays on the rehabilitation of society.

                    BUDDY
          I agree...

                    GUY
          Indeed.

                    BUDDY
          Well good day to you sir I must be
          off...

                    GUY
               (breaking character)
          No... No, it's me that must be
          off...

                    BUDDY
          Oh... Right... See you next time
          sir.. Have a good day!

                    GUY
          Ya see... That's all there is to
          it.

                    BUDDY
          Uh huh...

                    GUY
          Ya see, like this we can hope to
          live somewhat normal lives.

                    BUDDY
          Yeah, but what happens when the
          store runs out of food or the post
          office doesn't successfully deliver
          your letter?

                    GUY
          Well ya can't win 'em all, Buddy...
          We're just gonna have to take it
          one day at a time.

                    BUDDY
          Alright I guess you're right...
          It's been a long day as it is...

                    NARRATOR
          Buddy sees that Guy is stressing
          out and decides to try to cheer him
          up by playing along in his
          not-so-elaborate costume charades.

BUDDY
Hey... Uh, I forgot... I, uh, have to make it to the bank before it closes...

NARRATOR
Guy's face lights up with excitement as he hurries behind the counter and dons the banker attire.

GUY
Welcome to the Bunker-Bank, how can we disservice you today?

BUDDY
Yes I'd like to deposit this check, please.

GUY
Oh, that's gonna be a 10 dollar fee...

BUDDY
What?

GUY
10 dollar fee.. It's gonna be a 10 dollar fee for me to hang on to this deposit for ya.

BUDDY
Well that doesn't seem fair...

GUY
Well, do you know another bank in this bunker that'll deposit your check?

BUDDY
I guess I don't...

GUY
Well then if you have 10 dollars I suggest you cough it up...

NARRATOR
Buddy reluctantly rifles through his wallet and finds 10 dollars. Guy snatches it up and pockets it.

PAPER RUSTLE

> BUDDY
> Man, I thought banks were bad before the end of the world...

> GUY
> Here's your receipt. Your check will clear in 10 days...

> BUDDY
> 10 days!?

> GUY
> You in some kind of hurry to spend it... Not like the world's gonna end or anything...

> BUDDY
> (sarcastically)
> Ha. Ha.

> GUY
> Well my shift is over... Time to call it a day...

> NARRATOR
> Guy removes his attire and begins opening cans as if to make dinner.

CAN OPENER

DISHES

> BUDDY
> Well it's been a long day... I think I'd like to relax with a beer and a joint...

> GUY
> Go ahead ... I'll join you on that...

> NARRATOR
> Guy opens a cooler, cracks open 2 beers, and slides one to Buddy as he begins to roll a joint.

OPEN BEER CAN

DRINK SLIDE ON TABLE

> GUY
> I had a long day, myself.

BUDDY
Oh yeah, busy day at the bank?
(laughing at his joke)

GUY
You could say that again... I had this one asshole in there complaining about deposit fees... I told him, "If you can find another bank to cash your check in this bunker, you go right ahead!"

BUDDY
Ya don't say?

NARRATOR
Guy finishes plating food and slides it over to Buddy.

SILVERWARE CLATTER

GUY
You hungry? Dig in.

BUDDY
Canned ravioli... I love canned ravioli.

GUY
Good... my ex-wife back on the surface hated it.

BUDDY
Oh yeah, you were married once?

GUY
Oh yeah. For 10 years before we got divorced.

BUDDY
Ah that sucks, Guy...

GUY
Tell me about it...

NARRATOR
Buddy can see that this topic is emotional for Guy, so he decides to change the subject.

BUDDY
Hey what do ya say we turn the radio on, and see if we can pick up any signals?

GUY
Good call...

        END SILVERWARE CLATTER

NARRATOR
Buddy and Guy move over to the
shortwave radio and try to dial in
some frequencies.

        SHORT WAVE RADIO SOUNDS

BUDDY
Anything?

GUY
Nothing... Look, it's been a long
day... Maybe we should turn in
early?

NARRATOR
Guy has a worried look in his eye
and Buddy concurs.

BUDDY
I think maybe you're right...

NARRATOR
Guy shuts off the radio and dims
the lights.

        CUT OUT RADIO SOUND

        FADE OUT ENVIRONMENT

SCENE 3

        FADE IN MUSIC

NARRATOR
Scene 3...

        FADE OUT MUSIC

NARRATOR
It's been 2 years since Guy and
Buddy have met... Day after day
they tried to live a relatively
normal life through the use of
Guy's costumes and daily life
rituals... They grew close over the
years and began to disclose more
and more intimate things about
their lives to one another...

FADE IN ENVIRONMENT

GUY
So... You must be new to this bar... I never seen you in here.

BUDDY
Yeah, well I've lived in the area for years, I just never had the nerve to walk in until today.

GUY
Well it's a good thing you did because today only it's happy hour all day!

BUDDY
(laughing merrily)
Ha what do ya know, my lucky day... Pour me another drink!

NARRATOR
Guy pours Buddy another drink.

DRINK POUR AND GLASS CLINK

BUDDY
Hey, why don't you pour yourself one... On me... Come on, I got nobody to drink with.

GUY
Well ok, I suppose no one will know...

DRINKS POUR AND GLASSES CLINK

BUDDY
What should we toast to?

GUY
To peace on earth.

BUDDY
To peace on earth... Wow that's deep...

NARRATOR
Guy and Buddy tap glasses and suddenly realize the sadness of what they just toasted to.

GUY
(trying to change the subject)
Uh... So what... Uh... What did you say you used to do back on the surface?

BUDDY
Oh... I didn't do much... I was kind of an artist... Only ... I wasn't good at any art... I guess you could say the longest job I had was cleaning pools.

GUY
What did you just say?

BUDDY
I said I was a pool cleaner...

GUY
Really?

BUDDY
Yeah ,why do you ask? Ya got a pool at home that needs cleaned?

GUY
Well no... But back on the surface I did.

BUDDY
Oh yeah? Well, I probably cleaned your pool!

GUY
Yeah ya probably did, didn't ya? I thought you looked familiar?

BUDDY
Oh yeah, hows that?

GUY
Well, my wife--... I mean this friend of mine's wife... My friend the banker... Well, yeah, his wife left him for the pool guy...

NARRATOR
Buddy starts slowly realizing that he might be the very pool guy that his wife left him over.

BUDDY
Wait... Guy... I don't think that I'm the guy that you're--

GUY
LAST CALL!

BUDDY
Wait, what?

GUY
Last call, Buddy. better drink it up while you can. Bar's closing.

BUDDY
What happened to happy hour?... All day?

GUY
Happy hour's over. Look, I'm sorry, but I'm gonna have to cut you off. You look preee-etty drunk. You're gonna have to take a cab.

BUDDY
What happened to last call?

GUY
Sorry Buddy, your cab is here.

NARRATOR
Guy quickly puts on a taxicab hat and walks around the "bar" to the "door" and then enters the "bar."

GUY
Somebody call for a cab?

BUDDY
Um?... Yeah, I guess the cab's for me?

GUY
All right, let's go... We gotta hurry if were gonna beat rush hour home...

NARRATOR
Guy grabs four chairs and arranges them like that of an automobile. Buddy starts to get in the front seat.

                    GUY
I'm sorry no passengers in the
front seat... It's a safety risk.

                    BUDDY
Uh... Huh... Well I guess I'll just
get in the back here...

                    GUY
Where is it yer headed to?

                    BUDDY
Uh... Home, I guess.

                    GUY
Oh yeah? Got a nice home do ya?

                    BUDDY
Um.

                    GUY
I use to have a home... Back on the
surface... I had a home and wife
and dog and a beautiful daughter
and then, suddenly... My wife
decides to leave me... Said there
was no more passion in our
relationship... She left me for a
lousy pool cleaner who sold pot on
the side... You know what that kind
of pain is like? Do ya, huh!?

                    BUDDY
Look Guy... I'm sorry if I--

                    GUY
Here's yer stop... That'll be
$18.50.

                    BUDDY
$18.50?!... But I only been in the
car a moment...

                    GUY
Look Buddy, Don't give me a hard
time ok?... I got enough trouble as
it is... I lost my wife and kid and
house and dog in the apocalypse.

                    BUDDY
Oh yeah? We're not even at my house
yet. I'm not payin' full price for
half the ride.

                    GUY
You can get out and walk from here,
sir.

                    BUDDY
Walk? Are you crazy? I'm not givin'
you $18.50... Here I got 10 bucks,
That's more than enough...

                    GUY
Don't make me call the cops,
Buddy...

                    BUDDY
Cops?!... Yeah ya know what, go
ahead and call the cops...

                    NARRATOR
Guy calmly gets up and walks over
to the costumes, puts on the
policeman's cap, and grabs a billy
club and whistle...

                    GUY
Excuse me sir, would you please
step out of the vehicle...

                    BUDDY
Look... Guy... I know what this is
really about and I'm sorry... I'm
not even sure it's the same girl,
man.

                    GUY
Sir, I'm gonna have to ask you to
hand over the $18.50 you owe this
man... He has a receipt with him
showing that you owe him $18.50.

                    BUDDY
Oh, would ya just drop the charade
already...

                    NARRATOR
Buddy gets up and is instantly
pummeled by Guy's night stick,
knocking Buddy to the floor... Guy
continues to strike Buddy as he
grunts and groans in defense.

                                        FIGHT/STRUGGLE

                                        BODY THUMP

                    GUY
          It'll be a lot easier if you stop
          resisting, sir... Sir... Just...
          Just relax!

                                                    FIGHT/STRUGGLE

                    BUDDY
          Ok... Ok ... Ok you win... Here's
          the money... Keep the change...
          Good god, what the hell, Guy?

                    GUY
          Have a good day, sir...

                    NARRATOR
          Guy walks across the bunker, takes
          off his hat, and puts down his
          police attire... He strolls over to
          the table and chair where they eat
          and pours himself a drink.

                                                    DRINK POUR

                    BUDDY
          God... Ya didn't have to hit me so
          hard...

                    NARRATOR
          Guy does not respond or acknowledge
          Buddy... Buddy gets to his feet and
          limps over towards Guy.

                    BUDDY
          This shit is kind of getting out of
          control, Guy... We need to have a
          serious talk...

                    GUY
          You're right... We do need to
          talk... You know while you were out
          I saw my friend the bartender...
          And ya know what he told me?

                    BUDDY
          Oh my god.

                    GUY
          He told me some asshole came in the
          bar and got so drunk he had to cut
          him off... And then you know what
          he went on to say...

BUDDY
I think I kind of have a clue.

GUY
He said the drunk asshole went on to say he was a pool guy... Can you believe that?

BUDDY
Look... Guy... I didn't know--

GUY
You know my wife left me for a pool guy... Did I ever tell you that...

BUDDY
Well not directly no... But I--

GUY
Yeah, left me for a guy who cleans pools... How do you like that... What do you think the odds are of me running into a pool guy in this bunker, here?

BUDDY
Oh come on now, Guy, we don't even know it was the same woman, do we?... I mean I cleaned a lot of pools, ya know...

GUY
What was the name of that woman you were tellin' me about that was steppin' out on her husband and foolin' around with you?

BUDDY
Her name was Karen...

GUY
Oh yea... Ya know what my wife's name was?... It was Karen.

BUDDY
Look I'm sorry Guy... If I knew I was gonna be locked in a fallout shelter with you I would've never slept with your wife...

GUY
So you admit it?

                    BUDDY
I guess... I did... I had no
idea... I was just a dumb pool kid
and this hot older lady started
hitting on me.

                    GUY
You son of a--

                    NARRATOR
Guy punches Buddy in the face,
knocking him to the ground.

FACE PUNCH

BODY THUMP

                    BUDDY
Oh... I guess... I deserved that...

                    NARRATOR
Guy recoils his fist as if to punch
Buddy again... But Buddy looks up
with a look of terror in his eye.
Realizing maybe he's gone a bit
overboard, Guy begins to regret
what he's just done.

                    GUY
Look ... I'm sorry, Buddy... I
didn't mean to--

                    BUDDY
Stay away from me... You just stay
away from me, Guy.

                    GUY
I'm sorry Buddy... I didn't mean to
scare ya...

                    NARRATOR
Buddy fixes his hair and wipes the
blood and spit from his lower lip.
He walks over to his cot, picks up
a book, and starts writing in it.

                    GUY
What's that you're doing?

                    BUDDY
I'm writing...

GUY
I can see that. What are you writing?

BUDDY
I'm keeping a journal... Just in case anything happens to me...

GUY
Oh come on now, Buddy... It's not like that...

BUDDY
Just leave me alone and let me write in my journal.

GUY
Fine, you know what? I'm gonna keep a journal too...

BUDDY
Why? Nobody's gonna get a chance to read it.

GUY
Well not with that kind of attitude... I tell ya what... I'm gonna keep a journal too and we'll just see... Maybe my story will be turned into a best-seller when we get back on the surface.

NARRATOR
Buddy doesn't look up ... Guy has broken his trust... And they both know it. Buddy continues writing in his journal in silence.

GUY
Alright, well... It's been a long day so... I guess we should just retire to our journals... I'll get back on the radio tomorrow... Maybe we'll pick up some transmissions.

FADE OUT ENVIRONMENT

FADE IN MUSIC

SCENE 4

> **NARRATOR**
> Scene 4... Years pass as Guy and Buddy begin to grow paranoid of one another... Being locked up in a fallout shelter is starting to take its toll on them both mentally and physically. They both now have long beards.

FADE MUSIC OUT

> **NARRATOR**
> They continue living in fear of one another, rarely talking and keeping mostly to themselves, except to utter what can only be described as a series of grunts to convey thoughts to one another... Buddy and Guy take turns everyday trying to tune in radio signals on the shortwave radio...

ROLL IN RADIO SQUELCH SOUNDS

FADE IN ENVIRONMENT

> **NARRATOR**
> ... All the while still writing in their journals every night... It's been 4 years since they first locked themselves in the fallout shelter and the mental health of both men is starting to come undone. Guy is writing in his journal while Buddy searches for a signal on the radio.

SCRIBBLING/ PEN AND PAPER

ADD INTERNAL THOUGHT REVERB

> **GUY**
> (v.o. recording)
> It's been 4 years since I allowed him to enter the shelter with me... Looking back on it I realize it was a mistake... What am I suppose to do about that now?... I think about killing him in his sleep sometimes... But then every time I do, when I look over at him he

                    GUY
looks like he's thinking the same
thing, too, and I get spooked about
it...

                              CUT OUT SCRIBBLING

                    NARRATOR
Guy looks over at Buddy who seems
to be glaring at him... They both
quickly look away and Guy resumes
writing.

                              RESUME SCRIBBLING

                         ADD INTERNAL THOUGHT REVERB

                    GUY
              (v.o. recording)
No... I'm just paranoid...

                              CUT OUT SCRIBBLING

                    BUDDY
Uhhhhhg.

                    NARRATOR
Buddy grunts, indicating he's
frustrated with the lack of radio
signal coming in, and stands up to
take a break. Guy stops writing and
stands up to relieve Buddy from his
radio post.

                    GUY
Ehhh...

                    NARRATOR
Buddy grabs his book and pencil and
begins writing in his journal while
Guy dials in radio signals.

                              RADIO DIAL SQUELCH

                         SCRIBBLING/ PEN AND PAPER

                         ADD INTERNAL THOUGHT REVERB

                    BUDDY
              (v.o. recording)
I can't believe I have been locked
up with this maniac for 4 years now
and he hasn't killed me... I

                    BUDDY
suppose I could always go nuts and
kill him first...

                              CUT OUT SCRIBBLING

                    NARRATOR
Buddy stares daggers over at Guy on
the radio... Guy looks over his
shoulder and sees Buddy giving him
the stink eye. They both quickly
look away from each other.

                              RESUME SCRIBBLING

                         ADD INTERNAL THOUGHT REVERB

                    BUDDY
              (v.o. recording)
But I think to myself he might be
prepared for something like that
and I get nervous... God, how I
wish a signal would come through
that radio. We could really use a
rescue... I'm afraid Guy is losing
his mind... Rarely talks anymore
and furiously writes in his book
all the time... I know he's writing
hateful things about me...

                    NARRATOR
Guy grabs his journal off the desk
and acts like hes taking notes
about the radio.

                         ADD INTERNAL THOUGHT REVERB

                    GUY
              (v.o. recording)
God I hate that jerk so much... I
can't believe he slept with my wife
and he's living in MY bunker... Why
I'd kick 'em right out in the
fallout if I didn't think opening
the door would contaminate
everything in here... I should just
probably kill him before he kills
me...

                              CUT OUT SCRIBBLING

                    NARRATOR
Guy looks up from taking notes to
find that Buddy is already staring
at him... They quickly look away
again and go back to writing.

                              RESUME SCRIBBLING

                         ADD INTERNAL THOUGHT REVERB

                    BUDDY
              (v.o. recording)
I know he's up to something... And
ya know one thing that's been
driving me nuts... If he was gonna
be down here by himself... Why does
he have all these costumes down
here?... I mean, if I wasn't down
here then who the hell would he
have been playin' make-believe
with?... No doubt about it... This
guy is certifiably crazy...

                                 CUT SCRIBBLING

                    NARRATOR
Buddy looks up from his note-taking
just as Guy looks up from his notes
with an evil stare...

                              RESUME SCRIBBLING

                         ADD INTERNAL THOUGHT REVERB

                    GUY
              (v.o. recording)
I can't put my finger on it but I
swear he's recording my every
move... I wish I could read what
he's writing in his journal... He
sleeps with it every night, how
would I ever get it away from
him... I suppose I could kill him
in his sleep...

                                 CUT SCRIBBLING

                    NARRATOR
Guy looks up as if he's going to
look over his shoulder... Only this
time he doesn't ... Instead he goes
right back to writing.

RESUME SCRIBBLING

ADD INTERNAL THOUGHT REVERB

          GUY
      (v.o. recording)
What am I saying... I sound so paranoid... I keep having dreams about him and my wife ... I wake up drenched in sweat some nights... I can't take it anymore... I have to do something to end this silence... I think I have a plan to end it all... After all, I don't want all these costumes to go to waste.

CUT SCRIBBLING

          NARRATOR
Guy stops writing and stands up abruptly.

          GUY
Naaaahh.

          NARRATOR
Buddy understands that Guy is finished surfing the radio for the day and is turning in for the night by turning off the radio.

CUT OUT RADIO STATIC

          NARRATOR
Buddy goes back to writing in his journal.

RESUME SCRIBBLING

ADD INTERNAL THOUGHT REVERB

          BUDDY
      (v.o. recording)
How was I suppose to know HIS wife was Karen... It's not like I planned to get locked down here with the guy after I stole his woman... Still plenty enough reason to kill a man... I wonder why he hasn't killed me yet... I mean if it were me and I just so happened to let the guy who broke up my marriage in my fallout shelter, I'd definitely kill him...

                    NARRATOR
Buddy looks up at Guy one last time
who is also writing in his journal
on his bed returning the same evil
stare...

                                        CUT SCRIBBLING

                    GUY
Ehh?

                    BUDDY
Ehh...

                    NARRATOR
They both grunt in agreement that
they are going to sleep for the
evening... They both cover up as
Guy dims the lights.

                                        FADE OUT ENVIRONMENT

                                        FADE IN MUSIC

SCENE 5

                    NARRATOR
Scene 5... Buddy wakes up startled
to find Guy sitting at the table,
staring at him while he slept. Guy
has laid out in front of him a huge
breakfast.

                                        FADE OUT MUSIC

                                        FADE IN ENVIRONMENT

                    BUDDY
Uh...?

                    GUY
Look here, Buddy... I can't live
like this anymore... I just want
you to know... I forgive you for
what happened back on the
surface...

                    BUDDY
Really?

                    GUY
Yeah, look, I should have said this
years ago... I feel ashamed of the

GUY
way I treated you when I first found out... That's just not me... I dunno, I think being cooped up in this bunker has started gettin' to me.

BUDDY
Yeah, well, I can certainly understand that.

GUY
Look, I made you this breakfast because I want to say I'm sorry, and that I forgive you, and I want to let bygones be bygones... I miss having someone to talk to...

BUDDY
Alright... Well I guess it takes a strong man to apologize... I can respect that... Sure... I'd love to have breakfast with you, Guy.

NARRATOR
Buddy gets up off his bed and joins Guy at the table.

GUY
Put 'er there, Buddy

BUDDY
Thanks, Guy...

NARRATOR
The 2 men shake hands and exchange a look of mutual agreement for the first time in years.

BREAKFAST CLATTER

BUDDY
Oh boy... This breakfast looks fantastic... Are you sure we shouldn't save some of this?

GUY
No it's ok, I checked our supplies. We should be able to afford to enjoy this entire breakfast... I don't know how many more breakfasts we could do like this but I'm feeling exceptionally well this morning!

BUDDY
I'm glad you finally said something... I was beginning to miss conversation... I was starting to wonder if I would ever have another conversation again.

GUY
...Well, why would you wonder something like that?

BUDDY
Oh well... No ... Not like that... Just if we would ever get out of this bunker, ya know? And if we did, do you even think there's any survivors?

GUY
There has to be... There just has to be.

BUDDY
You know what, you're right... And I tell ya what... When we get back on the surface I wanna be lookin' good.

GUY
Oh yeah?

BUDDY
Yeah.

GUY
What are you tryin' to say?

BUDDY
I think you know what I'm tryin' to say.

GUY
I think I DO know what you're tryin' to say...

NARRATOR
They both hop up from the breakfast table enthusiastically and head toward the costumes... Buddy clears the chairs from in front of the counter and places a single chair in the middle of the room, then walks toward the entrance of the

NARRATOR
bunker, pretending to have just entered.

BUDDY
(in character)
Yes hello sir... I think I'd like a haircut and a shave if you're not too busy... Ya see... I haven't had a haircut or a shave in over 4 years because the world was destroyed, and well it turns out we might make it back on the surface some day and I--

GUY
(breaking character)
No dude... You're gonna be the barber first.

NARRATOR
Guy hands him the barber outfit in one hand and straight razor in the other... Buddy realizes that in handing him a straight razor he's just armed him with the most lethal tool in the whole bunker... Any previous thoughts that Buddy might have had about killing Guy has suddenly turned to guilt... If it wasn't for Guy, Buddy wouldn't be alive at all... And for that Buddy is humbled by the gesture... They give a long stare and a nod of agreement... As they switch identities.

BUDDY
(in character)
Hello sir, welcome to the fallout Mustachary! You look like you're well overdue for a shave!

GUY
Indeed I am, good barber, indeed I am... Ya see I haven't had shave in almost 5 years, and well, it turns out we might just live long enough to walk on the surface again. And if that's so, well, I wanna be lookin' good in case I run into any women that were genetically mutated in a voluptuous way, if you know what I mean...

NARRATOR
He motions at his chest like a woman with large breasts.

BUDDY
I think I do, good sir... Have a seat. You've come to the best barber in the entire fallout shelter... What kind of a cut would you like?

GUY
One that suits me best ....

BUDDY
Yes sir, right away sir...

NARRATOR
Buddy drapes the barber smock around Guy and begins to cut at his long beard with the scissors.

SCISSOR SNIPS

BUDDY
How long do you suppose before you walk on the surface?

GUY
Oh well at least another 2 years... So we have some time to get it right... The hair style, that is.

NARRATOR
The two share a forced ironic laugh with one another as they pick up where they left off years ago, before the paranoid years consumed them... The two were friends as if nothing happened... Years passed and before you knew it... Christmas was upon them...

FADE OUT ENVIRONMENT

FADE IN XMAS MUSIC

SCENE 6

                NARRATOR
Scene 6... It's been over 6 years since the two men sealed themselves in the fallout shelter and, all things considered, they're getting along extraordinarily well... The simple thought of walking on the surface and having their skin kissed by the sunrays once more keeps the fight alive in them... It's Christmas Eve and Guy is dressed like Santa. So the two are busy trimming the tree with gusto.

                FADE OUT XMAS MUSIC

                FADE IN ENVIRONMENT

                GUY
You see, now that's how ya decorate a tree, I tell ya what.

                BUDDY
You're right... And when you're right you're right... Only one thing...

                GUY
What's that?

                BUDDY
The popcorn... I hate when people string popcorn on the tree... It looks so out of place...

                GUY
How do ya mean?

                BUDDY
I mean what does popcorn have anything to do with Christmas or Jesus for that matter?

                GUY
Well, I'm not quite sure... I just always thought of it as more of a traditional thing.

                BUDDY
Well, it's a bad tradition that doesn't make any sense... Between

BUDDY
you and me... That's one of the reasons me and Karen didn't stay together.

GUY
What?

BUDDY
Yeah... One Christmas, the only Christmas we ever spent together... I woke up in the middle of the night and I was hungry and everything was wrapped up for Christmas the next day... So I ate some popcorn off the tree.

GUY
You did what?

BUDDY
I ate the popcorn off the tree... I didn't think it was a big deal... But when we woke up in the morning and she found evidence of popcorn crumbs all around the tree and missing popcorn... Well, she flipped out...

GUY
Well, I can see why... You didn't even wait till after presents to eat the popcorn?

BUDDY
Well no, I figured there were plenty of candy canes and other treats everyone could have enjoyed... Anyway, she flipped out about the popcorn and I was like... Anyone who takes this stupid tradition that serious is just not right for me.

GUY
So you left her over stringing popcorn on the tree?

BUDDY
Well not the popcorn, just the way she got so worked up over it... I'm a very non-confrontational lover ya understand... I couldn't deal with the stress.

                    GUY
I see.

                    NARRATOR
Guy has a moment of deep internal
conflict as he processes this
information.

                    GUY
Ya know what... Fuck the popcorn.

                    NARRATOR
Guy rips the popcorn off the tree.

                              CHRISTMAS TREE SHAKING

                    BUDDY
See... Much better... and now we
can eat this popcorn before it goes
stale and starts tasting like a
pine tree.

                    GUY
You're right... And when you're
right, you're right...

                    BUDDY
Agreed.

                    GUY
Say... Did you visit Santa and tell
him what you want?

                    BUDDY
What?... Well, no.

                    GUY
Oh well you better go right now!
It's almost midnight and it's
Christmas Eve!

                    NARRATOR
Guy grabs a coat and hands it to
Buddy, picking him up off his feet
and forcing him out the door...

                    GUY
Go, go, go ... Hurry up!

                    NARRATOR
Guy grabs a single chair, places it
in front of the Christmas tree, and
sits on it, facing Buddy.

GUY
Ho, Ho, Ho! Merry Christmas... Come sit on Santa's lap and tell him what you want for Christmas!

BUDDY
... Do I have to?

GUY
Ho, Ho, Huurrry up I don't have a lot of time, kid. There's a million other kids in bombshelters dying to see Santa... Now what do you want?

BUDDY
I don't know, maybe a steak dinner?

GUY
Why that's not very creative... Go ahead, tell Santa what you really want.

BUDDY
Ok you know what I really want?... I'd like to see the sun again... Or maybe breathe fresh air straight from the surface... Or how about snow? Ya think ya could use your Santa magic so I could see snow again... I mean, it is Christmas...

GUY
Snow?

BUDDY
Oh yeah, and if you feel like pullin' off any last minute Christmas miracles you could have a voice come over the emergency frequency just once...

NARRATOR
Guy takes his wishes to heart as he wishes for the very same things as Buddy... A look of excitement fills Guy's face as he says--

GUY
Well, have you been a good boy all year Buddy?

BUDDY
I mean... Yeah I guess I have ...

GUY
Well hurry home and just maybe you'll get one of your wishes.

BUDDY
Fat chance, Santa...

NARRATOR
Buddy hops up and walks to the exit and back, signaling he has come home.

GUY
Sooo... Did ya tell Santa what you wanted?

BUDDY
Yeah.

GUY
Well, what did he say?

BUDDY
He said the checks in the mail...

GUY
Ha, oh, that Santa... Oh hey... I got you something for Christmas... I know it's early but I can't wait any longer.

BUDDY
Um well... Ok.

GUY
Come over here ... I want to show you something I've kept secret.

NARRATOR
Buddy is very intrigued as he knows every inch of the bunker.

BUDDY
What is it?

GUY
Right over here... When I first built this bunker... I had a periscope put in... I don't know how airtight the seals are on it so

                    GUY
I never wanted to use it... Just in
case...

                    BUDDY
You mean you had this the whole
time and you never told me?

                    GUY
Yeah, well, like I said, I didn't
want to risk exposing our faces to
radiation... But under the
conditions and seeing how the 7
years are almost up... I guess it's
ok to take a peek... Maybe see if
it's snowing...

                    BUDDY
Ya mean it... You would do that for
me?

                    GUY
Hey, what are friends for? And
besides... I know how bad you wanna
see snow... I'll let you in on a
little secret... I'm the Santa at
the mall...

                    BUDDY
Ya don't say?

                    NARRATOR
Buddy looks at Guy with gratitude,
realizing he never talks about
"work" when he's at "home."

                    GUY
Go ahead. You do the honors...

                    NARRATOR
Buddy grabs the periscope with both
hands and Guy hits a button making
the periscope ascend.

                                            BUTTON SOUND

                                            MOTOR SOUND

                    BUDDY
Oh my god... I can see it... It's
snowing... !

                    NARRATOR
Spinning around in place, Buddy
whips the periscope around...

                    BUDDY
There it is ... The moon... I can
see the moonlight reflecting off
the snow...It's beautiful... I can
see shadows from naked trees on the
snow... It's glorious, Guy... You
have to look at this!

                    NARRATOR
Just then the radio begins to light
up and the static turns to
interference, then voices.

                                        RADIO STATIC

                                        RADIO SQUELCH

                    EMERGENCY FREQUENCY
                (woman v.o.)
pon pon... pon pon... This is the
United States Government hailing
frequency... is anyone receiving
this transmission... pon pon... pon
pon...

                    GUY
It's a rescue signal!...

                    BUDDY
It's a woman!

                    NARRATOR
Buddy and Guy look at each other in
amazement and rush over to the
radio to reply to the transmission.

                    GUY
Hello... pon pon... I mean, hello,
yes, we're receiving your
transmission. Over.

                    EMERGENCY FREQUENCY
                (woman v.o.)
This is the United States
Government hailing on all
frequencies... Is your party safe
and secure underground?

                    GUY
Yes... We're in a state-of-the-art bunker ... We've been sealed down here for almost 7 years and our supplies are running low...

            EMERGENCY FREQUENCY
              (woman v.o.)
Stand by.

                    BUDDY
Can you believe it, Guy!?... It's a Christmas miracle!

                    GUY
I know Buddy, I know.

            EMERGENCY FREQUENCY
              (woman v.o.)
Please check in at this frequency at 12 hundred hours every day... We will triangulate your location and send an extraction team in approximately... 9 weeks.

                    GUY
Read you loud and clear... Transmit at 1200 hours every day for 9 weeks... Over and out.

                    BUDDY
Wow... I can't believe it... Just 9 weeks left?... Do you know what that means?

                    GUY
We're gonna make it?

                    BUDDY
Yeah we're gonna make it! You did it, Guy... You survived the apocalypse...

                    GUY
Merry Christmas, Buddy.

                    BUDDY
Merry Christmas, Guy...

FADE OUT ENVIRONMENT

FADE IN MUSIC

SCENE 7

> **NARRATOR**
> Scene 7... It's the evening before the extraction team arrives and the anniversary of the day they sealed themselves in the fallout shelter. Both men are beaming with anticipation... Buddy is dressed up as a construction worker coming home from work.

FADE OUT MUSIC

FADE IN ENVIRONMENT

> **BUDDY**
> Knock, knock...

> **GUY**
> Oh, there you are... Long day at work?

> **BUDDY**
> Oh, you bet it was... So much construction stuff... Yep... Tomorrow when we get back on the surface it should be all fixed up for us...

> **GUY**
> Well, that's great news... I knew we could do it... And to celebrate I made us the finest food we have left.

> **BUDDY**
> What's that?

> **GUY**
> It's steaks and porkchops wrapped in bacon.

> **BUDDY**
> Sweet Jesus, it's beautiful...

> **GUY**
> Dig in ... I insist!

> **NARRATOR**
> Buddy flops down at the table and begins to cut at his steak.

                                        DISHES AND CUTTING SFX

             GUY
     But first... A toast.

                                        CUT OUT DISH CLATTER

             NARRATOR
     Guy stops Buddy and hands him a
     glass of red wine.

             BUDDY
     Why thank you... What should we
     toast to?

             GUY
     To seven years of fallout!

             BUDDY
     To seven years of fallout.

             NARRATOR
     They touch glasses and begin to
     drink.

                                        GLASSES CLINK

             NARRATOR
     Buddy takes a big gulp of wine and
     tries to savor the taste.

             BUDDY
     Oh my god, this wine is
     delicious... What year is this?

             GUY
     It was a good year, the year my
     wife left me... So you know...
     Should taste pretty bittersweet.
     (nervous chuckle)

             BUDDY
     Oh my god, it's to die for... I
     drank it all up in one gulp! Can I
     have another glass?

             GUY
     Please, I insist.

             NARRATOR
     Guy pours him another drink.

                                        DRINK POUR

BUDDY
You know what... I want to make a toast.

GUY
To what?

BUDDY
To you... To my good friend Guy who helped me survive the apocalypse... Without you... I would truly be dead...

GUY
Oh shucks, it was nothing... You would have done the same for me...

BUDDY
Ya see, that's just the thing... I don't know that I would have, Guy... Thanks for being the better man.

NARRATOR
Guy looks at Buddy and touches glasses with him.

GLASSES CLINK

GUY
CHEERS...

BUDDY
CHEERS...

NARRATOR
They have one last toast and Buddy begins to eat vigorously.

DISHES AND CUTTING SFX

GUY
Ya know Buddy, when we're finished with dinner I want to play a little game with you.

BUDDY
Oh yeah, like what? Like chess or checkers or something?

GUY
No, I had a different idea...

NARRATOR
Guy presents Buddy with 2 small bottles and in each bottle there is a pill.

BUDDY
What's that?

GUY
There are 2 bottles. In one bottle, cyanide. In the other is a harmless sugar pill... You choose a bottle, and whatever bottle you choose, I will eat the pill in the other bottle... And we'll both eat them together.

BUDDY
What?... Why would we do that?... The extraction team comes tomorrow... There is no reason for either of us to die at this point...

GUY
Well, surely when we get on the surface we'll have to repopulate the world, and I'm not trying to compete with any other alpha males.

BUDDY
Alpha male? What the hell are you talking about, man... I'm sure there's plenty of women when we get back on the surface... Hell, there may even be more women than men!

GUY
Either way, we're eatin' these pills and only one of us is making it out alive... So whats it gonna be?

BUDDY
What if I don't wanna play? What if I don't eat any pills... You gonna hit me again? Huh? You gonna kick my ass or even kill me this time?

GUY
No... Nothing like that.

BUDDY
Well then fine, I'm not playing.

GUY
Fine... Doesn't matter anyway because I already poisoned your food...

BUDDY
You did what?!

GUY
I poisoned your food.

BUDDY
Why the fuck would go and do a thing like that?!

GUY
Well because you fucked my wife!

BUDDY
That shit happened years ago... I thought you forgave me!

GUY
Well no... I only pretended to forgive you... Really I'm still pissed about the whole thing.

BUDDY
Well, then, why didn't you kill me years ago when you first found out?

GUY
I thought about that, too... Ya see the only reason I didn't was because if I DID... Well then, I would have been stuck down here with your rotting corpse for years... Wouldn't I?

BUDDY
So you let me live all these years... All that make-believe we did... Didn't that mean anything?

GUY
Well, yes, it did until you made that comment about the popcorn on the Christmas tree.

                    BUDDY
What? The fucking popcorn?

                    GUY
I LOVED STRINGING THE POPCORN UP WITH KAREN!... Some of my favorite memories of her, are of us stringing the popcorn on the tree.

                    BUDDY
You've got to be kidding me!

                    GUY
She was too good for you... You took her for granted... And ya see where that got ya, huh... Fuckin' dead, Buddy...

                    NARRATOR
Buddy begins to feel the effects of the poison.

                    GUY
And another thing I'd like to talk to you about... I found your journal, here...

                              BOOK THUMP ON TABLE
And I'm glad I read it because I found many entries where you talk about killing me in my sleep...

                    BUDDY
That shit was years ago!... I can't... I can't believe you let me live this long only to kill me the day before we're rescued...

                    GUY
Well ya can't win 'em all Buddy... Hey it could be worse.

                    BUDDY
HOW! How could it possibly be any worse!... I'm dyin' over here... And I'm never gonna see the surface again... The last 7 years of my life have been pointless...
(coughing)

                    GUY
Nah, I wouldn't say that... Remember that time we survived the apocalypse?

                    BUDDY
Real fuckin' cute, Guy...

                    NARRATOR
Just then a voice comes over the
radio.

                    EMERGENCY FREQUENCY
                    (woman v.o.)
pon pon... pon pon... This is the
United States Government fallout
extraction team... We have
triangulated your location and will
be arriving in less then one
hour... Please make your way into
the extraction chamber and wait for
the specialized extraction vehicle
to connect to your airlock... This
is the United States Government
fallout extraction team. pon pon
... pon pon...

                    GUY
Well looks like the big moment is
here... Do you have any last words
before we say goodbye?

                    BUDDY
I do...(coughing)... My only regret
... Is having ever met Karen
Boyle...

                    GUY
Wait. What did you just say?

                    BUDDY
Karen. I wish I never met her...
Because then I would have never
slept with your wife... And you
might not have poisoned me for
it...

                    GUY
No, I mean about the Karen part,
what did you say her last name was?

                    BUDDY
Boyle... Karen Boyle.

                    GUY
Oh ... Shit... I think I might have
made a mistake. Ya see, my
ex-wife's name was Karen Baker...

BUDDY
Huh?

GUY
Oh... Jeez man I'm sorry.

BUDDY
Are you kidding me? ... It's not the same Karen?

GUY
I guess not... Oh gosh ... I'm so sorry about the whole letting-you-live-only-to-kill-you-before-we-get-rescued thing... I hope you can forgive me...

BUDDY
ggggahhhh

NARRATOR
Just then Buddy takes his last gasp of air, collapses to the ground, and is indeed dead...

GUY
Aww man... What have I done...

EMERGENCY FREQUENCY
(woman v.o.)
pon pon...pon pon... This is the United States fallout shelter extraction team... We are at your location and attempting to connect to your airlock...

METALLIC DOOR THUMP

NARRATOR
Guy rushes over to the radio and responds.

GUY
Yes, I'm alive inside and waiting for extraction...

NARRATOR
Guy walks over to the costumes, puts on a HAZMAT suit, and takes one last look around the bunker... He pulls out a flashlight and shines it over at Buddy, then pretends to hold a walkie talkie up to his mouth.

                    GUY
chhhh... It seems they're all dead
down here Jim... Preparing to head
back to the extraction point...
chhhh...

                    NARRATOR
Guy turns off his flashlight and
begins to climb the ladder to the
surface... The sound of the
extraction team at the door echos
in the fallout shelter.

                                        METALLIC THUMPS

                                        CLIMBING LADDER

                                        AIR LOCK SOUND

                    EMERGENCY FREQUENCY
                         (v.o.)
This is the United States
Government extraction team... We
have securely connected to your
airlock. Please proceed into the
specialized extraction vehicle ...
I repeat please proceed to the
specialized extraction vehicle...

                    NARRATOR
The footsteps climbing up the
ladder grow faint as Guy exits the
shelter. The only survivor of the 7
years of fallout...

                                        FADE OUT VOICE

                                        FADE OUT FOOT STEPS

                                        FADE OUT ENVIRONMENT

                                        FADE IN MUSIC

-The End-

                    END CREDITS

                                        OUTRO MUSIC

                    NARRATOR
You have been listening to THE
CLEVELAND RADIO PLAYERS performance
of FALL OUT GUYS, written and

                        NARRATOR
directed by MILTON HOROWITZ,
narrated by Cory Shy, recorded at
BAD RACKET STUDIOS... Starring:

        LOGAN SMITH

        MILTON MATTHEW HOROWITZ

        DENNY CASTIGLIONE

        DEANNA DIONNE

        KAT BI

To listen to Fall Out Guys as a
radio play, please visit
www.clevelandradioplayers.com

Rights and Royalties

Originally adapted for the radio and performed by The Cleveland Radio Players

Directed by Milton Matthew Horowitz

Recorded at Bad Racket Studios

For more information on performance rights and royalties, or to listen to Fall Out Guys as a radio play, please visit www.ClevelandRadioPlayers.com